The Zen Leader:

How Meditation Can Transform Your Leadership Style

The Zen Leader:

How Meditation Can Transform Your Leadership Style

Great things in business are never done by one person, they are done by a team of people.

Andrew Attack

I would like to dedicate this book to my family:

My two children, Max and Roxy;
My Aunt Margaret;
My late parents, Shirley and John;
And my late sister, Hilary.

Self-published by Andrew Attack

Copyright © Andrew Attack 2024

The right of Andrew Attack to be identified as the owner of this work has been asserted in accordance with the Copyright, Designs and Patents Act, 1988.

All rights reserved. No part of this publication may be reproduced, stored in a retrieval system, or transmitted in any form or by any means, electronic, mechanical, photocopy, recording or otherwise without the prior permission in writing of the copyright holder, nor be otherwise circulated in any form of binding or cover other than in which it is published and without a similar condition being imposed on the subsequent publisher.

ISBN: 9798325593796

The information and ideas presented in this book are based on the author's personal experience. There is no guarantee that your experience will be the same or that you will have similar results.

Contents

Forward 11

Acknowledgements 15

Chapter 1: Introduction to Meditation for Leaders ..17

    Understanding the Connection Between Meditation and Leadership 17

    The Benefits of Incorporating Meditation into Your Leadership Style..19

    Common Misconceptions About Meditation for Business Leaders..21

Chapter 2: The Basics of Meditation 24

    Different Meditation Techniques for Leaders 24

    Setting Up a Meditation Practice for Busy Business Leaders 26

    Overcoming Common Challenges in Meditation...28

Chapter 3: Cultivating Mindfulness in Leadership 31

    The Role of Mindfulness in Effective Leadership...31

    Practicing Mindfulness in Daily Business Operations 33

Using Mindfulness to Improve Decision Making ...35

Chapter 4: Enhancing Emotional Intelligence Through Meditation 37

Understanding Emotional Intelligence in Leadership 37

Using Meditation to Develop Self-Awareness and Self-Regulation.. 39

Building Empathy and Social Skills Through Mindfulness Practices 41

Chapter 5: Leading with Compassion 43

The Importance of Compassion in Leadership 43

Cultivating Compassion Through Loving-Kindness Meditation 45

Applying Compassion in Team Management and Conflict Resolution.. 47

Chapter 6: Creating a Culture of Wellbeing in Your Organisation 50

Promoting Employee Wellbeing Through Meditation Programs.. 50

Fostering a Healthy Work-Life Balance for Yourself and Your Team... 52

Implementing Mindfulness Practices in the Workplace 54

Chapter 7: Sustaining Your Meditation Practice as a Leader 56

Overcoming Burnout and Stress Through Meditation 57

Finding Support and Accountability for Your Meditation Practice 59

Integrating Meditation into Your Leadership Legacy 61

Chapter 8: Conclusion 64

Reflecting on Your Meditation Journey as a Leader 64

The Future of Meditation in Business Leadership . 66

Final Thoughts on Transforming Your Leadership Style with Meditation 68

Forward

My management style has developed over many years in supervisory and management positions both in my paid work and in voluntary positions.

It all started for me at my first employer when I became a team leader after being with them around eighteen months. As I progressed though the company, I was able to learn skills which I am still using nearly forty years later. The most important of these was learning to lead with compassion and empathy.

Not only have I been a leader in the business world, but in my voluntary work I have also been a leader. In a branch of one national charity, I spent seven years as a duty manager. This involved looking after the branch and volunteers' welfare for a twenty four hour shift once a month. In another national charity, I was responsible for sixty volunteers. This involved juggling the coverage of many duties and keeping a fair spread across all the volunteers to keep them happy and covering all the duties. In many ways, this is harder than managing a large team in a business.

I also started my own charity teaching members of the public about life saving skills free of charge. Here I not only had to manage the charity, but also all of the volunteers.

Over the years I have learned more new skills from people that I have worked with, from courses and from studying. Many of these will be touched on as you read this book.

One skill that I started to learn from a friend that I did not initially think of applying to my management style was the art of meditation. As we produced videos for our YouTube channel, it started to become part of a way of life. As I continued to study for other skills, I started to realise that meditation was definitely a far more mainstream practice than I had realised. This was when I thought about not only including in my personal life but also in the way I worked as a manager.

Forward

During my work on some other books, it became clear to me that I needed to write this book first. The others will be coming, but this book became the priority.

The Zen Leader

Acknowledgements

There are too many people who have influenced me over the years to mention them all, but some require a special mention here.

The very first people to influence anyone are their parents. My parents, Shirley and John, instilled a sense of fairness and the ability to know right from wrong. They also taught me so many other life skills, but these are an important basis to management.

As I have already said in the forward, I quickly worked my way up through the first company that employed me. This also meant that I worked for several years directly with the Managing Director, Peter Hare. Peter taught me many important business skills which I still practice to this day.

Over the years, working as a volunteer in one national charity, I was introduced to many new ideas for leading other volunteers.

In my current job, a person who has had a major influence on me is Len Kemp who was my boss for a large proportion of the twenty-four years that I have been in post.

More recently, my friend Samantha taught me about meditation. This became such a new way of managing my ways of thinking that it had a major impact on my life. Over the years I learned more and more about meditation from her.

A turning point in my thinking was when I was sitting in a course led by Nick Staab and hearing him talk about meditation too. It then struck me that it was much more mainstream than I had realised, and I started to talk to many other people about it.

It struck me that not only should I practice this at home but practicing it at work would enhance the way I work and also enhance the way that I manage my team.

I would like to thank everyone who has taught and influenced me over the years and thank you for reading this book.

Andrew Attack

Chapter 1: Introduction to Meditation for Leaders

Understanding the Connection Between Meditation and Leadership

With today's fast-paced and ever-changing business world, effective leadership is crucial for success. While many leaders focus on developing their skills and knowledge, one often overlooked aspect of leadership is the practice of meditation. Meditation has been shown to have numerous benefits for leaders, including increased focus, clarity and emotional intelligence. This practice, once looked upon as not having a place in everyday life by many, is fast becoming accepted as necessary by many leaders.

But what is the connection between meditation and leadership? At its core, meditation is about cultivating a sense of mindfulness and presence. This ability to be fully present in the moment can be a powerful tool for leaders, allowing them to make more informed decisions, build stronger relationships with their teams and navigate challenging situations with grace and composure.

By incorporating meditation into their daily routine, business leaders can enhance their leadership style in numerous ways. For example, meditation can help leaders develop the ability to stay calm under pressure, making them better equipped to handle the stress and uncertainty that often comes with leadership roles. Additionally, meditation can improve a leader's ability to listen actively and empathetically, fostering better communication and collaboration within their team.

Furthermore, meditation can help leaders develop a greater sense of self-awareness, allowing them to identify their strengths and weaknesses more effectively. This self-awareness can lead to more authentic and compassionate leadership as leaders are better able to connect with and understand the needs of their team members.

In conclusion, the connection between meditation and leadership is a powerful one. By incorporating

Introduction to Meditation for Leaders

meditation into their daily routine, business leaders can cultivate the mindfulness, presence and self-awareness needed to excel in their roles. By embracing meditation as a tool for personal and professional growth, leaders can transform their leadership style and create a more positive and productive work environment for their teams.

The Benefits of Incorporating Meditation into Your Leadership Style

In today's fast-paced business environment, where stress and burnout are all too common, incorporating meditation into your leadership style can have numerous benefits both for you and your team. The practice of meditation has been shown to reduce stress, increase focus and concentration and improve overall well-being. As a business leader, these benefits can have a significant impact on your ability to make sound decisions, communicate effectively and inspire your team.

The Zen Leader

One of the key benefits of incorporating meditation into your leadership style is improved emotional intelligence. By taking the time to quiet your mind and focus on the present moment, you can develop a greater awareness of your own emotions and those of others. This increased emotional intelligence can help you better understand and connect with your team members, leading to stronger relationships and more effective collaboration.

Meditation can also help you cultivate a sense of calm and clarity in the face of uncertainty and change, which are common challenges in the business world. By regularly practicing meditation, you can train your mind to stay present and focused even in high-pressure situations. This can help you make better decisions, stay composed under stress and inspire confidence in your team.

Furthermore, incorporating meditation into your leadership style can help you foster a more positive and inclusive work environment. By leading by example and prioritising your own well-being, you can encourage your team members to prioritise self-care and mental health as well. This can lead to a more

Introduction to Meditation for Leaders

engaged and motivated team, as well as lower rates of burnout and turnover.

Overall, the benefits of incorporating meditation into your leadership style are numerous and far-reaching. By taking the time to cultivate a regular meditation practice, you can become a more mindful, empathetic and effective leader, leading to better outcomes for both you and your team.

Common Misconceptions About Meditation for Business Leaders

As business leaders, the concept of meditation may seem foreign or even intimidating. However, it is important to debunk some common misconceptions surrounding meditation to fully understand its benefits for leaders in the business world.

One of the biggest misconceptions about meditation for business leaders is that it is a waste of time. Many may feel that they are too busy to sit still and meditate, believing that they could be using that time to work on more pressing matters. However, studies have shown that meditation can actually increase productivity and focus, making it a valuable use of time for busy leaders.

Another misconception is that meditation is only for those who are spiritual or have a specific belief system. In reality, meditation is a secular practice that can be beneficial for anyone, regardless of their religious or spiritual beliefs. It is simply a tool for training the mind and cultivating mindfulness, which can be applied to any aspect of life, including business leadership.

Some business leaders may also believe that meditation is only for those who are struggling with stress or mental health issues. While meditation can certainly be helpful in managing stress and anxiety, it is also a powerful tool for enhancing creativity, decision-making and emotional intelligence, all of which are critical skills for effective leadership.

By dispelling these common misconceptions about meditation, business leaders can open themselves up to the transformative power of this practice. Through

Introduction to Meditation for Leaders

regular meditation, leaders can cultivate a sense of calm and clarity that will not only benefit their own well-being but also positively impact their teams and organisations.

Chapter 2: The Basics of Meditation

Different Meditation Techniques for Leaders

In today's fast-paced and demanding business environment, effective leadership is more important than ever. As a business leader, you are constantly faced with challenges and decisions that can impact the success of your organisation. One powerful tool that can help you navigate these challenges with grace and clarity is meditation.

Meditation is not just for monks and spiritual seekers; it is a valuable practice that can benefit anyone, especially leaders. By incorporating meditation into your daily routine, you can cultivate a sense of calm, focus and self-awareness that will enhance your leadership skills and improve your decision-making abilities.

There are many different meditation techniques that can help you become a more effective leader. One

The Basics of Meditation

popular technique is mindfulness meditation, which involves focusing on the present moment and observing your thoughts and emotions without judgment. This can help you develop greater self-awareness and emotional intelligence, which are essential qualities for effective leadership.

Another powerful meditation technique for leaders is loving-kindness meditation, which involves cultivating feelings of compassion and kindness towards yourself and others. This practice can help you develop empathy and connect more deeply with your team, fostering a more positive and collaborative work environment.

Body scan meditation is another effective technique for leaders, as it involves systematically focusing on distinct parts of the body and releasing tension and stress. This can help you relax and recharge, allowing you to approach challenges with a clear and calm mind.

By exploring different meditation techniques and finding the ones that resonate with you, you can enhance your leadership skills and cultivate a more mindful and compassionate approach to leading your team. Incorporating meditation into your daily routine can help you become a more effective and resilient leader, capable of navigating the complexities of the business world with grace and poise.

Setting Up a Meditation Practice for Busy Business Leaders

In today's fast-paced business world, finding time for self-care and reflection can be challenging for busy leaders. However, incorporating a meditation practice into your daily routine can have profound benefits for both your personal well-being and your leadership style. Here are some tips for setting up a meditation practice that fits seamlessly into your busy schedule:

1. Start small: If you are new to meditation, do not feel overwhelmed by the idea of sitting in silence for lengthy periods of time. Start with just a few minutes each day and gradually increase the duration as you become more comfortable.

2. Find a quiet space: Creating a designated meditation space in your office or home can help you establish a routine and eliminate distractions. Choose a comfortable chair or cushion to sit on and make sure the area is free from noise and clutter.

3. Set a schedule: Consistency is key when it comes to meditation. Try to meditate at the same time each day, whether it is first thing in the morning before work or during your lunch break. Setting a specific time for your practice will help you make it a priority.

4. Use technology: If you struggle to stay focused during meditation, consider using guided meditation apps or podcasts to help you stay on track. These resources can provide structure and support for your practice, especially if you are new to meditation.

5. Be patient: Meditation is a skill that takes time to develop, so be patient with yourself as you navigate the difficulties of your practice. Remember that even a few minutes of meditation each day can have a positive impact on your well-being and leadership style.

By incorporating these tips into your daily routine, you can create a meditation practice that works for you as a busy business leader. With consistent effort and dedication, you will soon experience the transformative power of meditation in your personal and professional life.

Overcoming Common Challenges in Meditation

In the fast-paced world of business, meditation has become an essential tool for leaders to navigate the challenges of leadership with clarity, focus and resilience. However, like any practice, meditation comes with its own set of challenges that can hinder progress and growth. In this section, we will explore some common challenges that business leaders face in their meditation practice and provide strategies to overcome them.

The Basics of Meditation

One of the most common challenges to meditation is the inability to quiet the mind. In a world filled with constant distractions and responsibilities, it can be difficult to find the time and space to sit quietly and focus on the present moment. To overcome this challenge, business leaders can start by setting aside dedicated time each day for meditation, even if it is just a few minutes. By creating a routine and committing to a regular practice, leaders can train their minds to become more focused and present.

Another challenge that business leaders often face to meditation is dealing with discomfort or restlessness. Sitting still for an extended period can be physically and mentally challenging, especially for those accustomed to constantly moving and multitasking. To overcome this challenge, leaders can experiment with different meditation techniques, such as walking meditation or body scan meditation, to find a practice that is comfortable and sustainable for them.

Lastly, one of the biggest challenges to meditation for business leaders is finding the motivation to practice consistently. With busy schedules and demanding responsibilities, it can be easy to prioritise other tasks over meditation. To overcome this challenge, leaders can remind themselves of the benefits of meditation, such as increased focus, creativity and emotional intelligence. By setting clear goals and intentions for their practice, leaders can stay motivated and committed to their meditation practice.

Overall, by acknowledging and addressing these common challenges to meditation, business leaders can cultivate a more mindful and effective leadership style that benefits both themselves and their organisations.

Chapter 3: Cultivating Mindfulness in Leadership

The Role of Mindfulness in Effective Leadership

In the fast-paced and often stressful world of business leadership, the role of mindfulness cannot be understated. Mindfulness, the practice of being fully present and aware in the moment, has been shown to have a wide range of benefits for leaders, from increased focus and clarity to improved decision-making and emotional intelligence. In fact, many successful business leaders credit their practice of mindfulness with helping them to navigate the challenges of leadership with grace and resilience.

One of the key ways that mindfulness can impact leadership effectiveness is by helping leaders to manage stress and avoid burnout. In today's hyper-connected world, it is all too easy for leaders to become overwhelmed by the constant demands of their roles. By cultivating a mindfulness practice, leaders can learn to recognise the early signs of stress and take steps to address them before they escalate. This not only benefits the leader personally, but also has a positive impact on their team and organisation as a whole.

Mindfulness also plays a crucial role in developing emotional intelligence, which is essential for effective leadership. By tuning into their own thoughts and feelings, leaders can gain a deeper understanding of themselves and their motivations, as well as develop greater empathy and compassion for others. This heightened emotional intelligence allows leaders to build stronger relationships with their team members, inspire trust and loyalty and resolve conflicts more effectively.

Overall, the practice of mindfulness can be a powerful tool for business leaders looking to enhance their leadership skills and create a more positive and productive work environment. By incorporating mindfulness into their daily routine, leaders can improve their focus, decision-making and emotional intelligence, ultimately becoming more effective and inspiring leaders.

Cultivating Mindfulness in Leadership

Practicing Mindfulness in Daily Business Operations

In today's fast-paced business world, it can be easy to get caught up in the chaos and lose sight of what truly matters. However, by incorporating mindfulness practices into your daily business operations, you can not only reduce stress and improve focus but also enhance your leadership skills and overall effectiveness.

Mindfulness is the practice of being fully present and aware in the moment, without judgment. By cultivating this mindset in your daily business operations, you can learn to respond to challenges with calmness and clarity, rather than reacting impulsively out of fear or stress.

One way to practice mindfulness in your leadership role is to start each day with a short meditation or breathing exercise. This can help you centre yourself and set a positive tone for the day ahead. Throughout the day, take moments to pause and check in with yourself, noticing any tension or distractions that may be hindering your focus. By acknowledging these feelings without judgment, you can release them and refocus on the task at hand.

Additionally, practicing mindfulness can help you become more attuned to the needs and emotions of your team members. By actively listening and being present in your interactions, you can foster stronger relationships and create a more supportive and collaborative work environment.

Incorporating mindfulness into your daily business operations may require some initial effort and practice, but the benefits are well worth it. By cultivating a more mindful approach to leadership, you can enhance your decision-making abilities, improve communication with your team and ultimately become a more effective and compassionate leader.

Using Mindfulness to Improve Decision Making

In the fast-paced world of business, making decisions quickly and effectively is crucial for success. However, the pressure and stress of leadership can often cloud our judgment and lead to poor decision making. This is where mindfulness can play a crucial role in improving our ability to make sound decisions.

Mindfulness is the practice of being fully present and aware of our thoughts, feelings and surroundings. By cultivating mindfulness, business leaders can enhance their decision-making skills in several ways. Firstly, mindfulness helps to clear the mind of distractions and allows leaders to focus on the task at hand. This increased focus enables them to consider all relevant information and perspectives before making a decision.

Furthermore, mindfulness can help business leaders to regulate their emotions and reactions, leading to more rational and balanced decision making. Instead of reacting impulsively to a situation, leaders who practice mindfulness can take a step back, assess the situation calmly and choose the best course of action.

Additionally, mindfulness can help business leaders to tune into their intuition and gut feelings, which are often valuable sources of insight when making decisions. By being more in tune with their inner selves, leaders can tap into their intuition and make decisions that align with their values and goals.

Overall, incorporating mindfulness practices into their daily routine can help business leaders become more effective decision-makers. By cultivating mindfulness, leaders can develop a greater sense of clarity, focus and emotional regulation, leading to more thoughtful and strategic decision making in the fast-paced world of business.

Chapter 4: Enhancing Emotional Intelligence Through Meditation

Understanding Emotional Intelligence in Leadership

Emotional intelligence is a crucial component of effective leadership. It encompasses the ability to recognise and regulate one's own emotions, as well as understand and empathise with the emotions of others. In the fast-paced world of business, where decisions must often be made quickly and under pressure, emotional intelligence can make all the difference to how leaders navigate challenges and inspire their teams.

Meditation plays a key role in developing emotional intelligence in leadership. By cultivating mindfulness through regular meditation practice, business leaders can become more self-aware and better equipped to manage the ups and downs of the business world.

Meditation helps leaders to remain calm and focused, even in the face of adversity, allowing them to make better decisions and communicate effectively with their team members.

Understanding emotional intelligence in leadership also involves recognising the impact of emotions on decision-making and team dynamics. Leaders who are emotionally intelligent are able to create a positive work environment where team members feel valued and motivated. They are also better equipped to resolve conflicts and foster collaboration among team members.

In today's competitive business landscape, the ability to lead with emotional intelligence is a valuable skill that can set leaders apart from their peers. By incorporating meditation into their leadership style, business leaders can enhance their emotional intelligence and become more effective at guiding their teams towards success. Ultimately, understanding emotional intelligence in leadership is about creating a work culture that values empathy, self-awareness and effective communication. These are qualities that are essential for driving innovation

Enhancing Emotional Intelligence Through Meditation

and achieving sustainable growth in the business world.

Using Meditation to Develop Self-Awareness and Self-Regulation

In the fast-paced and high-pressure world of business leadership, it can be easy to lose sight of yourself amidst the demands of the job. However, through the practice of meditation, you can develop both self-awareness and self-regulation, ultimately transforming your leadership style for the better.

Meditation offers a powerful tool for increasing your self-awareness by allowing you to tune into your thoughts, emotions and physical sensations. By taking the time to sit quietly and observe your inner workings without judgment, you can gain valuable insights into your motivations, triggers and patterns of behaviour. This heightened self-awareness can help you better understand how you are seen as a leader and identify areas for growth and improvement.

Furthermore, meditation can also help you develop self-regulation, which is essential for effective leadership. By learning to cultivate a sense of calm and presence through meditation, you can better manage stress, navigate challenging situations with grace and make more thoughtful decisions. This ability to regulate your emotions and responses not only benefits your own well-being but will also positively impact your team and organisation.

By incorporating meditation into your daily routine, you can strengthen your leadership skills and become a more mindful, empathetic and effective leader. As you deepen your self-awareness and enhance your self-regulation through meditation, you will be better equipped to lead with clarity, compassion and authenticity. Take the time to invest in yourself through meditation and watch as your leadership style transforms for the better.

Enhancing Emotional Intelligence Through Meditation

Building Empathy and Social Skills Through Mindfulness Practices

In today's fast-paced business world, the ability to connect with others on a deeper level is becoming increasingly important for effective leadership. This is where mindfulness practices can play a crucial role in helping business leaders develop empathy and social skills.

By incorporating mindfulness techniques into their daily routines, business leaders can cultivate a greater sense of self-awareness and emotional intelligence. This heightened awareness allows them to better understand their own emotions and reactions, as well as those of their colleagues and employees. This, in turn, leads to improved communication, conflict resolution and overall team dynamics.

One of the key benefits of mindfulness practices is their ability to help individuals regulate their emotions and respond more skilfully in challenging situations. By learning to pause and observe their thoughts and feelings without judgment, business leaders can avoid impulsive reactions and make more thoughtful decisions. This not only fosters a more positive work environment but also enhances the leader's credibility and influence within the organisation.

Furthermore, mindfulness practices can help business leaders develop a greater sense of empathy towards others. By actively listening and being fully present in interactions, leaders can better understand the perspectives and needs of their team members. This fosters a culture of trust and collaboration, leading to increased employee engagement and productivity.

In conclusion, building empathy and social skills through mindfulness practices is essential for modern business leaders looking to enhance their leadership style. By incorporating these techniques into their daily routines, leaders can cultivate a greater sense of self-awareness, emotional intelligence and empathy towards others, ultimately leading to more effective and fulfilling leadership experiences.

Chapter 5: Leading with Compassion

The Importance of Compassion in Leadership

In today's fast-paced and competitive business world, many leaders are constantly striving to improve their skills and stay ahead of the curve. While traditional leadership qualities such as decisiveness, strategic thinking and communication skills are essential, one often overlooked quality that can truly set a leader apart is compassion.

Compassion is the ability to empathise with others, understand their perspectives and act with kindness and understanding towards them. In the context of leadership, compassion can have a profound impact on how a leader interacts with their team, clients and stakeholders. When leaders show compassion, they create a more positive and inclusive work environment, where team members feel valued and supported.

Research has shown that compassionate leaders are more likely to inspire trust and loyalty in their teams, leading to higher levels of employee engagement and productivity. In addition, leaders who demonstrate compassion are better equipped to manage conflicts and challenges, as they are able to see the bigger picture and consider the needs and perspectives of all stakeholders involved.

Integrating meditation practices into your leadership style can help cultivate compassion by promoting self-awareness, emotional intelligence and mindfulness. By taking the time to reflect on your thoughts and feelings, you can develop a greater sense of empathy and understanding towards others. Meditation can also help you stay calm and centred in high-pressure situations, allowing you to respond to challenges with compassion and grace.

Ultimately, the importance of compassion in leadership cannot be overstated. By embracing compassion as a core value in your leadership style, you can create a more positive and harmonious work environment, build stronger relationships with your team and ultimately achieve greater success in your business endeavours.

Cultivating Compassion Through Loving-Kindness Meditation

In the fast-paced and often cutthroat world of business, it can be easy to lose sight of our compassionate nature. However, cultivating compassion is not only essential for our own well-being but also for our effectiveness as leaders. One powerful tool for developing compassion is loving-kindness meditation.

Loving-kindness meditation, also known as Metta meditation, is a practice that involves sending loving-kindness and goodwill to ourselves and others. By focusing on positive emotions such as love, compassion and empathy, we can train our minds to be more compassionate and understanding towards ourselves and those around us.

For business leaders, incorporating loving-kindness meditation into their daily routine can have a profound impact on their leadership style. When we approach our interactions with colleagues, employees and clients from a place of compassion, we create a more positive and supportive work environment. This, in turn, can lead to increased productivity, creativity and employee satisfaction.

Moreover, cultivating compassion through loving-kindness meditation can help business leaders navigate challenging situations with grace and empathy. By developing a deeper sense of connection and understanding with others, we can foster stronger relationships and build trust within our teams.

In "The Zen Leader: How Meditation Can Transform Your Leadership Style," readers will learn practical techniques for incorporating loving-kindness meditation into their leadership practice. Through guided meditations and mindfulness exercises, business leaders can harness the power of compassion to become more effective, authentic and resilient leaders in today's competitive business world.

Applying Compassion in Team Management and Conflict Resolution

In the fast-paced world of business, effective team management and conflict resolution are essential skills for any successful leader. One often overlooked tool in a leader's arsenal is compassion. By applying compassion in team management and conflict resolution, leaders can create a more harmonious and productive work environment.

Compassion is the ability to empathise with others, understand their emotions and act with kindness and understanding. When leaders approach their team members with compassion, they build trust and create a sense of psychological safety that encourages open communication and collaboration.

In team management, leaders can use compassion to inspire and motivate their team members. By taking the time to understand each team member's unique strengths, weaknesses and motivations, leaders can tailor their management style to bring out the best in everyone. Compassionate leaders also recognise the importance of work-life balance and support their team members in finding harmony between their professional and personal lives.

When conflicts arise within a team, leaders can use compassion to navigate demanding situations with empathy and understanding. By actively listening to all parties involved and considering their perspectives, leaders can help mediate conflicts and find solutions that benefit everyone involved. Compassionate leaders also model healthy conflict resolution strategies for their team members, creating a culture of respect and cooperation.

Incorporating meditation practices into leadership can enhance a leader's ability to cultivate compassion. Meditation helps leaders develop self-awareness, emotional intelligence and a sense of inner calm that can be invaluable in challenging situations. By regularly practicing meditation, leaders can strengthen their ability to approach team management and conflict resolution with compassion and mindfulness.

Overall, applying compassion in team management and conflict resolution can transform a leader's approach to leadership and create a more positive and productive work environment for everyone involved. As business leaders embrace the power of compassion, they can inspire their teams to reach new heights of success and fulfilment.

Chapter 6: Creating a Culture of Wellbeing in Your Organisation

Promoting Employee Wellbeing Through Meditation Programs

In today's fast-paced and high-stress business environment, promoting employee wellbeing has become a top priority for business leaders. One effective way to support the mental and emotional health of your team is through meditation programs.

Meditation has been shown to reduce stress, increase focus and productivity and improve overall mental wellbeing. By incorporating meditation programs into your workplace, you can create a more positive and harmonious work environment that fosters creativity and innovation.

One of the key benefits of meditation for leaders is its ability to enhance self-awareness and emotional intelligence. Through regular meditation practice, leaders can cultivate a greater sense of clarity, empathy and compassion, which can lead to more effective decision-making and communication.

Implementing meditation programs in the workplace can also help to reduce absenteeism and turnover rates, as employees who are supported in their wellbeing are more likely to feel engaged and satisfied in their roles. This can ultimately lead to a more productive and successful organisation.

As a business leader, it is essential to lead by example and prioritise your own wellbeing in order to effectively promote the wellbeing of your team. By incorporating meditation into your own daily routine, you can demonstrate the importance of self-care and mindfulness to your employees.

Overall, promoting employee wellbeing through meditation programs is a powerful way to create a more positive and productive work environment. By investing in the mental and emotional health of your team, you can foster a culture of wellbeing and resilience that will benefit both your employees and your organisation as a whole.

Fostering a Healthy Work-Life Balance for Yourself and Your Team

In today's fast-paced business world, it can be easy to let work consume every aspect of our lives. As business leaders, it is crucial to prioritise maintaining a healthy work-life balance not only for ourselves but also for our teams. By fostering a healthy work-life balance, we can create a more productive, engaged and satisfied workforce.

Meditation is a powerful tool that can help us achieve this balance. By incorporating meditation into our daily routines, we can reduce stress, increase focus and clarity and improve our overall well-being. As leaders, it is important to lead by example and show our teams the benefits of incorporating meditation into their own lives.

One way to foster a healthy work-life balance for ourselves and our teams is to encourage regular breaks throughout the workday. Encourage your team members to take short breaks to practice mindfulness or meditation. This can help them recharge and come back to work with renewed energy and focus.

Another important aspect of maintaining a healthy work-life balance is setting boundaries. As leaders, it is important to establish clear expectations around work hours and availability. Encourage your team members to disconnect from work outside of office hours and prioritise self-care activities.

By fostering a healthy work-life balance for ourselves and our teams, we can create a more positive and productive work environment. Incorporating meditation into our leadership style can help us achieve this balance and lead our teams with clarity, focus and compassion. As business leaders, it is essential to prioritise our well-being and the well-being of our teams in order to achieve long-term success.

Implementing Mindfulness Practices in the Workplace

As business leaders, it is essential to recognise the importance of mindfulness practices in the workplace. In today's fast-paced and high-stress work environments, incorporating meditation and mindfulness techniques can have a transformative impact on both individual leaders and their teams. By embracing mindfulness practices, leaders can cultivate a greater sense of clarity, focus and emotional intelligence, which are crucial qualities for effective leadership.

One of the key benefits of mindfulness practices is the ability to manage stress and improve overall well-being. By incorporating regular meditation sessions or mindfulness exercises into your daily routine, you can reduce feelings of overwhelm and anxiety, leading to a more balanced and centred approach to your work. This, in turn, can have a positive ripple effect on your team, creating a more harmonious and productive work environment.

Creating a Culture of Wellbeing in Your Organisation

In addition to stress management, mindfulness practices can also enhance your leadership skills by increasing self-awareness and empathy. By taking the time to cultivate a deeper understanding of your thoughts, emotion and reactions, you can become more attuned to the needs and perspectives of your team members. This heightened sense of awareness can improve communication, foster trust and strengthen relationships within your organisation.

To successfully implement mindfulness practices in the workplace, it is essential to lead by example. Make a commitment to prioritise your own well-being and set aside time each day for meditation or mindfulness exercises. Encourage your team members to join you in these practices and create a supportive environment where everyone feels comfortable exploring the benefits of mindfulness.

By incorporating mindfulness practices into your leadership style, you can cultivate a more mindful and compassionate approach to your work, leading to greater clarity, focus and effectiveness as a leader. Embrace the transformative power of meditation and mindfulness and watch as your leadership style evolves to new heights of success and fulfilment.

Chapter 7: Sustaining Your Meditation Practice as a Leader

Overcoming Burnout and Stress Through Meditation

In today's fast-paced and competitive business world, burnout and stress have become all too common among business leaders. The pressure to constantly perform, meet deadlines and navigate challenging situations can take a toll on even the most seasoned professionals. However, meditation is a powerful tool that can help business leaders overcome burnout and stress.

Meditation has been practiced for centuries as a way to calm the mind, reduce stress and increase focus and clarity. It is a simple yet effective practice that can be incorporated into even the busiest of schedules. By taking just a few minutes each day to sit quietly and focus on your breath, you can begin to cultivate a sense of inner peace and balance that will help you navigate the difficulties of leadership with grace and ease.

One of the key benefits of meditation for business leaders is its ability to help you stay present and focused in the midst of chaos. By learning to quiet the mind and tune into the present moment, you can avoid getting caught up in worry about the future or regret about the past. This can help you make better decisions, communicate more effectively and lead with confidence and clarity.

Meditation can also help you cultivate a sense of resilience and perspective that will serve you well in the face of challenges and setbacks. By learning to observe your thoughts and emotions without judgment, you can develop a greater sense of self-awareness and emotional intelligence, which are essential qualities for effective leadership.

In "The Zen Leader: How Meditation Can Transform Your Leadership Style," you will learn practical techniques for incorporating meditation into your daily routine and overcoming burnout and stress. By taking the time to nurture your inner well-being, you

Sustaining Your Meditation Practice as a Leader

can become a more effective and inspired leader who can navigate the complexities of the business world with grace and ease.

Finding Support and Accountability for Your Meditation Practice

In the fast-paced world of business leadership, finding time for self-care practices like meditation can often fall by the wayside. However, incorporating meditation into your daily routine can have numerous benefits for your leadership style, including increased focus, reduced stress and improved decision-making abilities. But how can you ensure that you stay committed to your meditation practice in the midst of your busy schedule?

One key strategy is to find support and accountability for your meditation practice. This can come in many forms, from joining a meditation group or class to working with a meditation coach or mentor. By surrounding yourself with like-minded individuals who are also committed to their meditation practice, you can create a sense of community and encouragement that will help keep you motivated and on track.

Another way to find support and accountability for your meditation practice is to set specific goals and milestones for yourself. By establishing clear objectives for your meditation practice, you can track your progress and stay motivated to continue meditating regularly. You can also enlist the help of a trusted colleague or friend to hold you accountable and check in on your progress.

Remember, finding support and accountability for your meditation practice is not a sign of weakness, but rather a smart strategy for ensuring that you prioritise your well-being and personal growth as a leader. By seeking out support from others and setting clear goals for your meditation practice, you can cultivate a sense of mindfulness and presence that will positively impact your leadership style and effectiveness.

Sustaining Your Meditation Practice as a Leader

Integrating Meditation into Your Leadership Legacy

As business leaders, it is crucial to understand the power of meditation in transforming your leadership style and leaving a positive legacy. By incorporating meditation practices into your daily routine, you can cultivate the qualities of a Zen leader - one who is calm, focused and compassionate in the face of challenges.

Meditation can help you develop self-awareness, emotional intelligence and resilience, all of which are essential traits for effective leadership. By taking the time to pause, breathe and centre yourself through meditation, you can better manage stress, make clearer decisions and communicate more effectively with your team.

Incorporating meditation into your leadership legacy means setting an example for those around you and creating a culture of mindfulness within your organisation. By demonstrating the benefits of meditation through your own actions, you can inspire others to prioritise their well-being and personal growth.

One way to integrate meditation into your leadership legacy is to start each day with a short mindfulness practice. Whether it is a few minutes of deep breathing, a guided meditation, or a simple body scan, taking the time to centre yourself before diving into your work can set a positive tone for the rest of the day.

Additionally, consider incorporating mindfulness practices into team meetings or retreats to foster a sense of connection and collaboration among your employees. By creating space for reflection, empathy and open communication, you can cultivate a more harmonious and productive work environment.

In conclusion, by integrating meditation into your leadership legacy, you can cultivate a more mindful, resilient and compassionate approach to leading others. Through your own practice and example, you can inspire those around you to prioritise their well-being and personal growth, ultimately creating a

Sustaining Your Meditation Practice as a Leader

more positive and sustainable work culture for the future.

Chapter 8: Conclusion

Reflecting on Your Meditation Journey as a Leader

As a business leader, it is essential to take time to reflect on your meditation journey and the impact it has had on your leadership style. Meditation is a powerful tool that can transform the way you lead others, allowing you to cultivate greater focus, clarity and emotional intelligence. By reflecting on your meditation practice, you can gain valuable insights into how it has influenced your decision-making, communication and overall effectiveness as a leader.

One of the key benefits of meditation for leaders is its ability to help you stay grounded and present in the midst of chaos and uncertainty. Through regular practice, you can learn to quiet the noise of your mind and connect with your inner wisdom, enabling you to make more informed and thoughtful decisions. Reflecting on how meditation has helped you

Conclusion

navigate challenging situations can provide you with a deeper understanding of your own strengths and limitations as a leader.

Furthermore, meditation can enhance your ability to connect with others on a deeper level, fostering stronger relationships and trust within your team. By reflecting on the ways in which meditation has improved your communication skills and empathy, you can identify areas for growth and continue to develop your emotional intelligence as a leader.

In conclusion, taking time to reflect on your meditation journey as a leader can be a powerful way to gain insight into the ways in which it has transformed your leadership style. By cultivating mindfulness and self-awareness through meditation, you can become a more effective and compassionate leader, inspiring those around you to reach their full potential.

The Future of Meditation in Business Leadership

The future of meditation in business leadership is filled with promise and potential. As more and more business leaders recognise the benefits of incorporating mindfulness practices into their leadership style, we are witnessing a shift towards more conscious and compassionate leadership strategies.

Meditation has been shown to reduce stress, improve focus and enhance emotional intelligence, all essential qualities for effective leadership. By taking the time to quiet the mind and cultivate self-awareness, leaders are better equipped to make sound decisions, communicate effectively and inspire their teams.

In the fast-paced and often chaotic world of business, meditation offers a much-needed pause for reflection and renewal. By incorporating regular meditation practice into their daily routine, leaders can cultivate

Conclusion

a sense of calm and clarity that allows them to navigate challenges with grace and resilience.

Furthermore, meditation can help business leaders foster a more inclusive and collaborative work environment. By developing empathy and compassion through mindfulness practices, leaders can build stronger relationships with their teams and create a culture of trust and respect.

As the benefits of meditation become more widely recognised, we can expect to see a greater emphasis on mindfulness in leadership development programs and corporate training initiatives. Companies that prioritise the well-being of their leaders and employees through meditation and mindfulness practices are likely to see improvements in productivity, creativity and overall performance.

In conclusion, the future of meditation in business leadership is bright. By embracing the power of mindfulness, business leaders can transform their leadership style and create more positive and impactful organisations. The time is now to unlock the full potential of meditation for leaders and usher in a new era of conscious and compassionate leadership.

Final Thoughts on Transforming Your Leadership Style with Meditation

As business leaders, we are constantly faced with challenges, stress and the pressure to perform at our best. It can be easy to get caught up in the chaos of the business world and lose sight of our true purpose as leaders. This is where meditation can be a powerful tool in transforming your leadership style and helping you become a more effective and mindful leader.

Through the practice of meditation, you can cultivate a sense of calm and clarity that will allow you to make better decisions, communicate more effectively and inspire your team to reach new heights. By training your mind to be more present and focused, you can develop the ability to lead with compassion, empathy and authenticity.

Conclusion

Meditation can also help you become more resilient in the face of adversity and uncertainty. By learning to observe your thoughts and emotions without judgment, you can develop a greater sense of self-awareness and emotional intelligence. This inner strength will enable you to navigate the challenges of leadership with grace and confidence.

Incorporating meditation into your daily routine can have a profound impact on your leadership style and the success of your organisation. By taking the time to quiet your mind and connect with your inner wisdom, you can tap into a source of creativity and intuition that will guide you in making wise and strategic decisions.

Remember, leadership is not just about achieving results, it is about inspiring and empowering others to be their best selves. By embracing the practice of meditation, you can transform your leadership style and create a more harmonious and fulfilling work environment for yourself and your team. Take the time to cultivate mindfulness and compassion in your leadership journey and watch as your organisation thrives under your guidance.

www.ingramcontent.com/pod-product-compliance
Lightning Source LLC
Chambersburg PA
CBHW050017230526
45470CB00003B/1004